This diary belongs to

____

and tells the story of my holiday to

____

which started on

____

and lasted for _____ days.

Welcome to your diary!

You are about to go on a wonderful holiday filled with excitement, fun and laughter. You might even make some new friends!

Record it all in here so that when you get back you can read all about it as often as you like!

Who I am going with:

Let's get excited! What are you really looking forward to about your holiday?

I can't wait to:

Make sure you remember to take everything you need.

Write it all down here.

What I will take:

Don't forget your friends and family at home. They will want to know all about your holiday when you get back, but it is also nice to let them know that you are thinking about them while you are away. List them all here and tick them off as you send your postcards, messages or e-mails.

Who I will send a message to:

Name	Sent

Think about where you are going. What do you want to do when you are there?

Things I want to do on holiday:

Your holiday sounds so exciting! Use this blank page to draw a picture of what you think it will be like.

The journey there.

Don't forget to write about the exciting journey to your holiday!

How did you travel?

How long did it take?

What did you like best?

What did you think when you arrived?

How excited were you?

Use this page for photographs

Use this page for photographs

My Holiday Diary

Day 1

Write anything you like here.

If you haven't filled the page, why not write something about these things:

Where did you go?

What did you do?

Did anything funny happen today?

Did you eat anything nice?

Did you meet anyone new?

How much did you enjoy the day?

Day 1 – Date:

My Holiday Diary

Day 2

Write anything you like here.

If you haven't filled the page, why not write something about these things:

Where did you go?

What did you do?

Did anything funny happen today?

Did you eat anything nice?

Did you meet anyone new?

How much did you enjoy the day?

Day 2 – Date:

Use this page for photographs

Use this page for photographs

My Holiday Diary

Day 3

Write anything you like here.

If you haven't filled the page, why not write something about these things:

Where did you go?

What did you do?

Did anything funny happen today?

Did you eat anything nice?

Did you meet anyone new?

How much did you enjoy the day?

Day 3 – Date:

My Holiday Diary

Day 4

Write anything you like here.

If you haven't filled the page, why not write something about these things:

Where did you go?

What did you do?

Did anything funny happen today?

Did you eat anything nice?

Did you meet anyone new?

How much did you enjoy the day?

Day 4 - Date:

Use this page for photographs

Use this page for photographs

My Holiday Diary

Day 5

Write anything you like here.

If you haven't filled the page, why not write something about these things:

Where did you go?

What did you do?

Did anything funny happen today?

Did you eat anything nice?

Did you meet anyone new?

How much did you enjoy the day?

Day 5 - Date:

My Holiday Diary

Day 6

Write anything you like here.

If you haven't filled the page, why not write something about these things:

Where did you go?

What did you do?

Did anything funny happen today?

Did you eat anything nice?

Did you meet anyone new?

How much did you enjoy the day?

Day 6 - Date:

My Holiday Diary

Day 7

Write anything you like here.

If you haven't filled the page, why not write something about these things:

Where did you go?

What did you do?

Did anything funny happen today?

Did you eat anything nice?

Did you meet anyone new?

How much did you enjoy the day?

Day 7 - Date:

Use this page for photographs

Use this page for photographs

My Holiday Diary

Day 8

Write anything you like here.

If you haven't filled the page, why not write something about these things:

Where did you go?

What did you do?

Did anything funny happen today?

Did you eat anything nice?

Did you meet anyone new?

How much did you enjoy the day?

Day 8 - Date:

My Holiday Diary

Day 9

Write anything you like here.

If you haven't filled the page, why not write something about these things:

Where did you go?

What did you do?

Did anything funny happen today?

Did you eat anything nice?

Did you meet anyone new?

How much did you enjoy the day?

Day 9 – Date:

My Holiday Diary

Day 10

Write anything you like here.

If you haven't filled the page, why not write something about these things:

Where did you go?

What did you do?

Did anything funny happen today?

Did you eat anything nice?

Did you meet anyone new?

How much did you enjoy the day?

Day 10 – Date:

Use this page for photographs

Use this page for photographs

My Holiday Diary

Day 11

Write anything you like here.

If you haven't filled the page, why not write something about these things:

Where did you go?

What did you do?

Did anything funny happen today?

Did you eat anything nice?

Did you meet anyone new?

How much did you enjoy the day?

Day 11 – Date:

My Holiday Diary

Day 12

Write anything you like here.

If you haven't filled the page, why not write something about these things:

Where did you go?

What did you do?

Did anything funny happen today?

Did you eat anything nice?

Did you meet anyone new?

How much did you enjoy the day?

Day 12 - Date:

Use this page for photographs

Use this page for photographs

My Holiday Diary

Day 13

Write anything you like here.

If you haven't filled the page, why not write something about these things:

Where did you go?

What did you do?

Did anything funny happen today?

Did you eat anything nice?

Did you meet anyone new?

How much did you enjoy the day?

Day 13 – Date:

My Holiday Diary

Day 14

Write anything you like here.

If you haven't filled the page, why not write something about these things:

Where did you go?

What did you do?

Did anything funny happen today?

Did you eat anything nice?

Did you meet anyone new?

How much did you enjoy the day?

Day 14 – Date:

The journey home.

This is not always the most exciting part of your holiday, but one day you will want to read about it, so write it down here.

The journey home

Use this page for photographs

Use this page for photographs

When you get home, keep thinking about your holiday. You will remember it for the rest of your life!

The best things about my holiday were:

Did you make any new friends on holiday? If so, why not write their names here so you can remember them.

Friends I made on holiday

Printed in Great Britain
by Amazon.co.uk, Ltd.,
Marston Gate.